OFFICIAL SQA PAST PAPERS WITH ANSWERS

INTERMEDIATE 2

GEOGRAPHY
2006-2009

First exam published in 2006.
Published by Bright Red Publishing Ltd, 6 Stafford Street, Edinburgh EH3 7AU
tel: 0131 220 5804 fax: 0131 220 6710 info@brightredpublishing.co.uk www.brightredpublishing.co.uk

ISBN 978-1-84948-043-7

A CIP Catalogue record for this book is available from the British Library.

Bright Red Publishing is grateful to the copyright holders, as credited on the final page of the book, for permission to use their material.
Every effort has been made to trace the copyright holders and to obtain their permission for the use of copyright material.
Bright Red Publishing will be happy to receive information allowing us to rectify any error or omission in future editions.

INTERMEDIATE

2006

[BLANK PAGE]

X208/201

NATIONAL
QUALIFICATIONS
2006

MONDAY, 29 MAY
9.00 AM – 11.00 AM

GEOGRAPHY
INTERMEDIATE 2

Candidates should answer **four** questions: Section A   Question 1
and
Question 2

AND
Section B   any **two** questions from
Questions 3 to 7

Candidates should read the questions carefully. Answers should be clearly expressed and relevant.

Credit will always be given for appropriate sketch-maps and diagrams.

Write legibly and neatly, and leave a space of about one cm between the lines.

All maps and diagrams in this paper have been printed in black only: no other colours have been used.

SCOTTISH
QUALIFICATIONS
AUTHORITY

©

1:25 000 Scale
Explorer Series

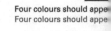

Four colours should appe
Four colours should appe

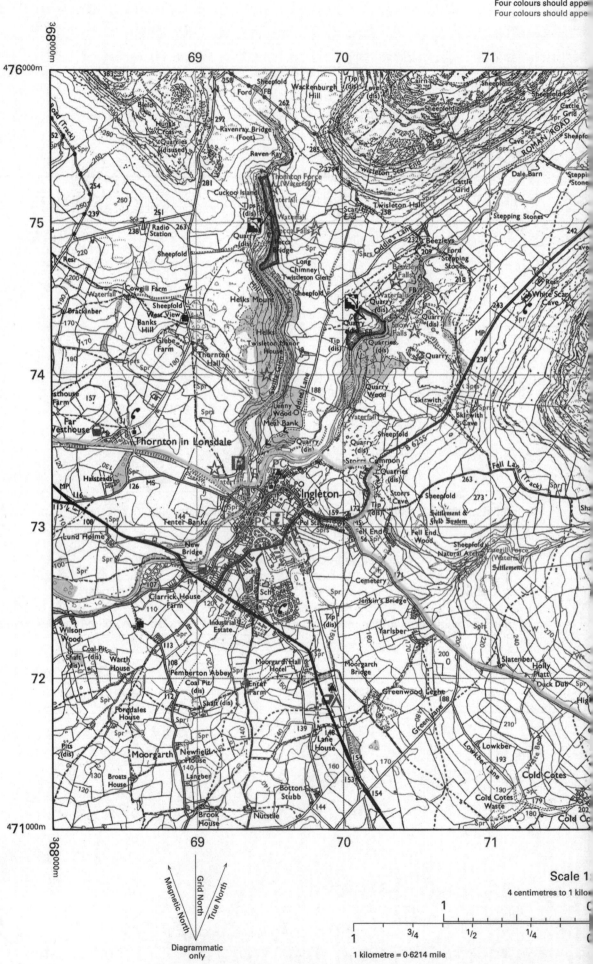

Magnetic North   Grid North   True North

Diagrammatic
only

Scale 1

4 centimetres to 1 kilo

1   3/4   1/2   1/4

1 kilometre = 0·6214 mile

Extract No 1490/OL2

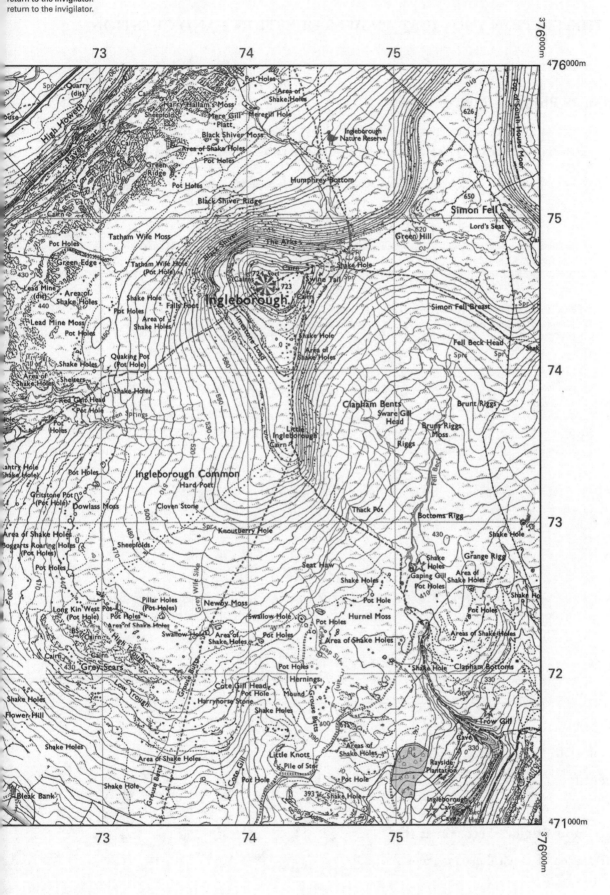

1 Mile = 1·6093 kilometres

Marl

SECTION A

IN THIS SECTION YOU <u>MUST</u> ANSWER QUESTION 1 <u>AND</u> QUESTION 2.

Question 1: Physical Environments

Reference Map Q1A: Selected Scenic Areas in the British Isles

(a) Look at Reference Map Q1A.

Identify:

(i)   the river at A;

(ii) area of glacial erosion at B;

(iii) area of coastal erosion at C.

3

Marks

1. **(continued)**

Reference Diagram Q1B: Cross section from Thornton Hall GR 690742 to White Scar Cave GR 716745

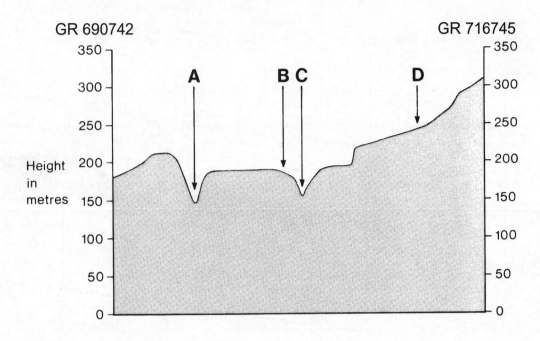

(b) Look at the Ordnance Survey Map.

Study Reference Diagram Q1B which shows a cross section from grid reference 690742 to 716745.

Using the OS Map, match the letters (A, B, C and D) on the cross section above with the correct feature below.

River Doe   Woodland Trust   B6255   River Twiss   3

[Turn over

Mark

1. (continued)

Reference Diagram Q1C: An Area of Upland Limestone

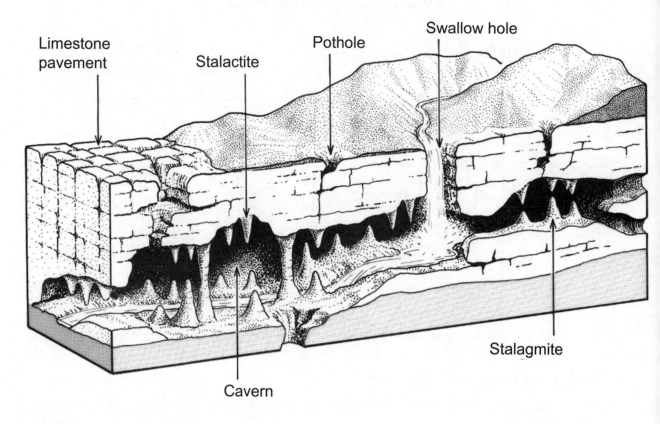

(*c*) Study Reference Diagram Q1C above.

Choose **one surface** limestone feature and **one underground** limestone feature from the diagram and **explain** how each was formed.   **6**

(*d*) Using **map evidence**, explain the **economic** and **environmental** impact which quarrying may have on the area of the map extract.   **5**

Marks

1. **(continued)**

Reference Diagram Q1D: Land Uses in an Area of Upland Glaciation

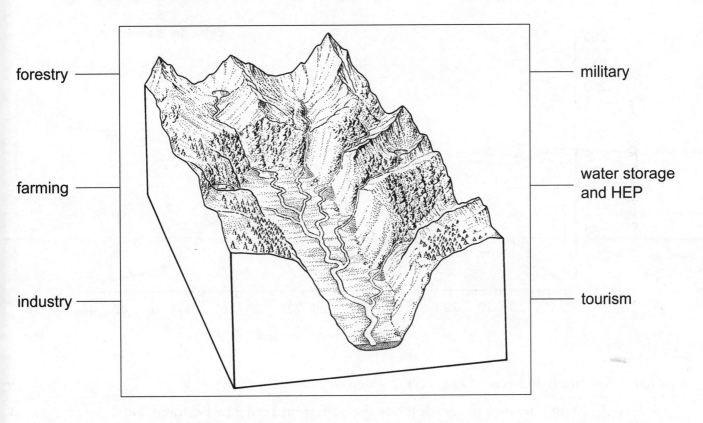

forestry

farming

industry

military

water storage and HEP

tourism

(e) Study Reference Diagram Q1D.

  (i) For an area of upland glaciation you have studied, select **two land uses** from the Reference Diagram and **explain** how they are in conflict with each other.   **4**

  (ii) Referring to the land use conflict discussed in part (i), describe **in detail** measures which can be taken to deal with the conflict.   **4**

  (25)

[END OF QUESTION 1]

NOW GO ON TO QUESTION 2

Tourism & Forestry are in conflict with each other in an area such as a glaciated upland. Forestry schemes want to protect and look after the enviroment. Whereas Tourists don't keep to footpaths and can end up damaging the forest enviroment.

To help stop the effects of tourism, there could be stronger punishments for people who dont stick to foot paths. There could be more policies made in order to protect the forestry areas.

Mark

Question 2: Human Environments

Reference Diagram Q2A: Births per 1000 Women 1951 and 2001, Europe

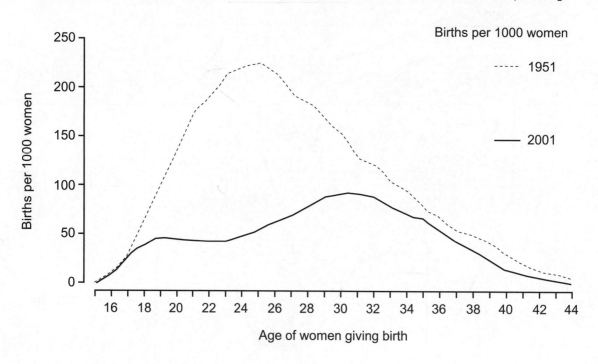

(*a*)   (i)   Study Reference Diagram Q2A above.

With reference to age, describe the pattern of births in 1951 and 2001.   **3**

(ii) **Suggest reasons** for the changes in the pattern of births per 1000 women between 1951 and 2001. • *Lack of contreception in 1951 in comparison to*   **3**
2001.

(iii)   **Reference Diagram Q2B**

In 1951 there

> **"By the time these young people turn 60, things will not be so rosy."**
>
> **Quote by Government spokesperson**

was overall a lot more women giving birth, because there was less acess to contreception. Between age 17 and 24 the birth per 1000 women rised from 50 to nearly 250. The amount of births decreased between the age of 25-44. In 2001 there was alot less births and was more spread out over all ages, peaking slightly at the age of 30.

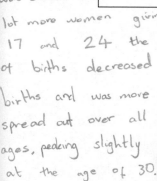

2. **(*a*) (iii) (continued)**

Reference Diagram Q2C: Population Changes for Scotland 2002–2042

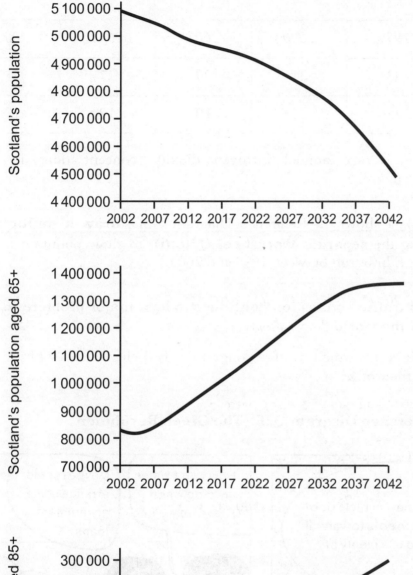

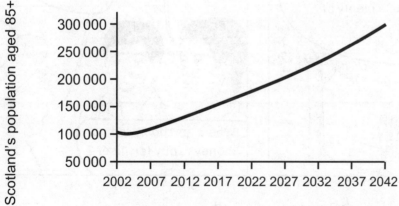

(iii) Study Reference Diagrams Q2B and Q2C above.

Explain the implications of these population changes for Scotland by the year 2042.

4

[Turn over

Mar

2.   **(continued)**

Reference Diagram Q2D: Pollution Levels in London and Edinburgh

	1999	*2000*	*2001*	*2002*	*2003*
London	33	31	29	27	25
Edinburgh	25	21	19	19	17

(Measurements show average annual nitrogen dioxide concentrations in $\mu g/m^3$ (micrograms per cubic metre).)

(*b*)   (i)   Using the data shown in Reference Diagram Q2D, **draw a multiple line graph**, using the **separate Worksheet Q2(*b*)(i)**, to show pollution levels in London and Edinburgh between 1999 and 2003.   3

(ii)   **"Increased traffic congestion continues to be a major problem in cities throughout the world."**

Describe ways in which traffic congestion is being dealt with in cities throughout the world.   3

Reference Diagram Q2E: The Green Revolution

(*c*)   Study Reference Diagram Q2E.

For an area which you have studied within an Economically Less Developed Country (ELDC), **describe** the advantages and disadvantages of the **Green Revolution**.   4

Marks

2.   (continued)

Reference Diagram Q2F: Changes in the Use of the Site of the former Ravenscraig Steel Works, North Lanarkshire

Location map of the former Ravenscraig site which closed in 1992.

Ravenscraig after demolition.

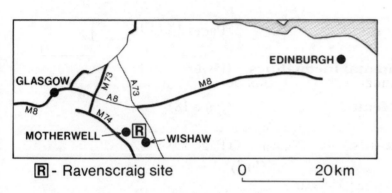

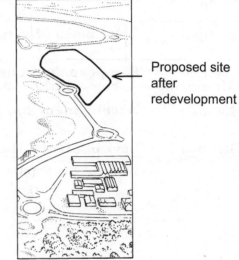

As manufacturing declines, service based industries increase.

A £20 million "shoppertainment" retail park is set to replace former steel works. It will include shops, offices, sports facilities and houses.

(*d*) Study Reference Diagram Q2F.

The former site of the Ravenscraig Steel Works in North Lanarkshire is a redevelopment area.

What are the advantages and disadvantages of building a large "shoppertainment" retail park in this area?

5

(25)

[*END OF SECTION A*]

NOW TURN TO SECTION B AND ANSWER TWO QUESTIONS

SECTION B

Environmental Interactions

Answer any two questions from this section.

Choose from

Marks

SECTION B

Question 3: Rural Land Degradation

Reference Diagram Q3A: Deforestation in Rondonia, Brazil

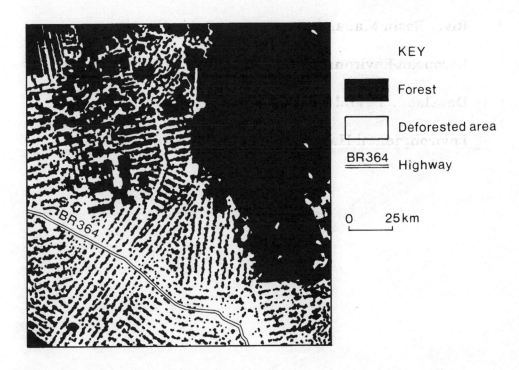

KEY

Forest

Deforested area

BR364 Highway

0   25 km

(*a*) Study Reference Diagram Q3A above.

Describe the environmental effects of increased deforestation in Rondonia or any
other forest area you have studied.   5

[Turn over

Mar

3.   **(continued)**

Reference Diagram Q3B: Sahel Region

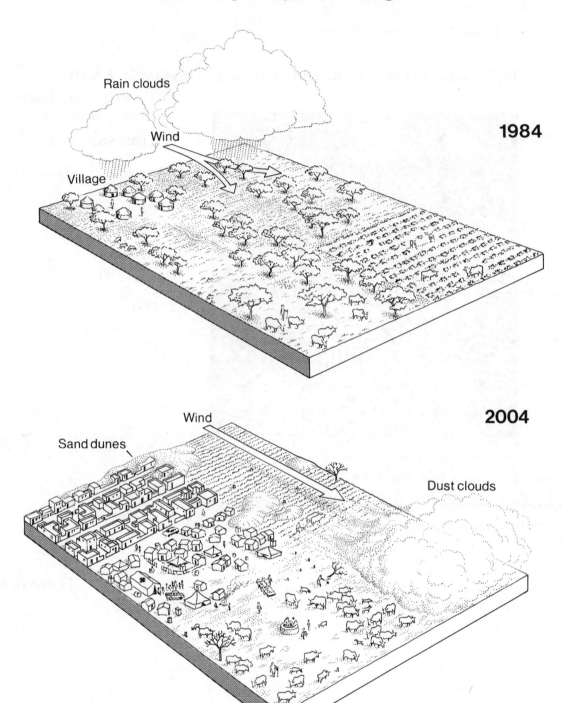

(b) Study Reference Diagram Q3B.

   (i) **Explain** ways in which both **physical** and **human** factors contribute to increased desertification in areas such as the Sahel region of Africa.   6

   (ii) For an area you have studied, comment on the effectiveness of the methods chosen to tackle the causes of desertification.   4

(15)

Question 4: River Basin Management

Reference Diagram Q4A: A Model Drainage Basin

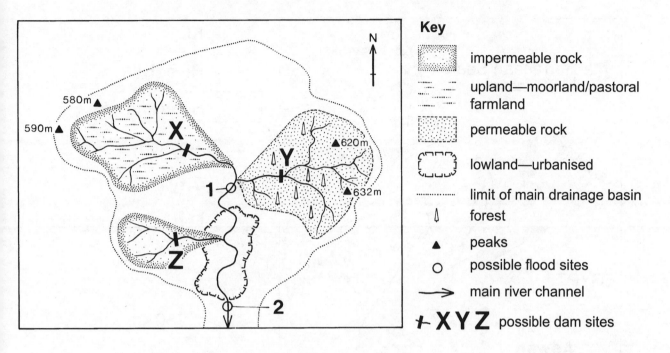

Key

(dotted)	impermeable rock
(dashed)	upland—moorland/pastoral farmland
(stippled)	permeable rock
	lowland—urbanised
....	limit of main drainage basin
⇓	forest
▲	peaks
○	possible flood sites
→	main river channel
+ X Y Z	possible dam sites

(a) (i) Study Reference Diagram Q4A.

The diagram above shows three possible sites for a new dam.

Which site would be the most suitable for a water management scheme? Give **reasons** for your answer.   4

(ii) Study Reference Diagram Q4A.

"Surface features can affect run-off".

If there was a prolonged period of heavy rainfall, which of the two points, 1 or 2, on the river, is most likely to flood? Give **reasons** for your answer.   3

[Turn over

4. (continued)

Reference Diagram Q4B: Location Map of the Nile and Aswan Dam

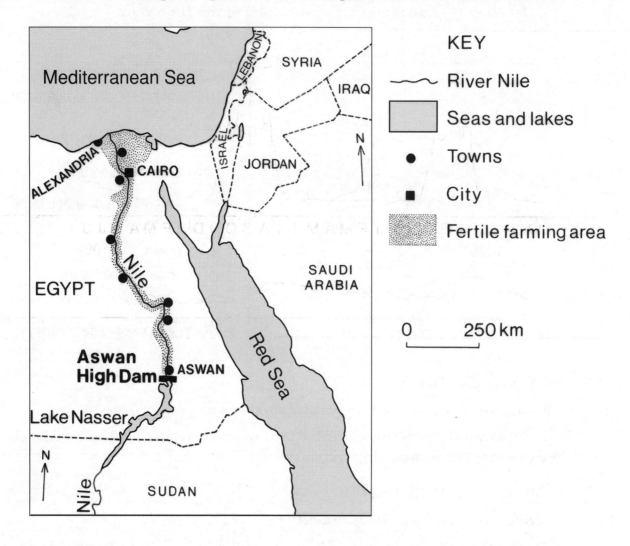

Reference Diagram Q4C: Quote from Government Spokesperson in the 1950s

"The amount of water in the Nile is subject to wide seasonal variations, with 80% of the annual total received during the flood season."

Marks

4.   (continued)

Reference Diagram Q4D: Monthly Volume of Water in the River Nile at Aswan, before (A) and after (B) Construction of the High Dam

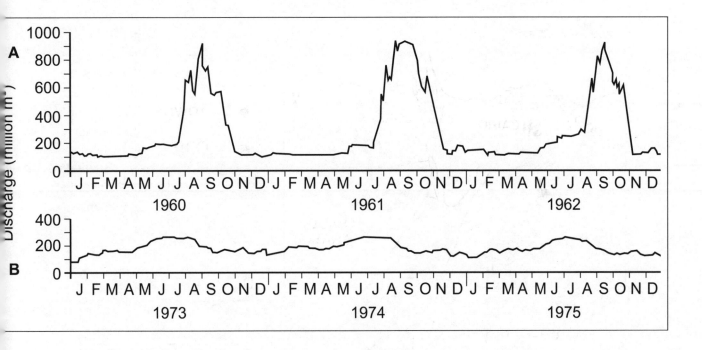

(b) Study Reference Diagrams Q4B, Q4C and Q4D.

"The Aswan High Dam was built in the 1960s."

(i)   Describe the benefits of this dam for people living between Aswan and Alexandria.   4

(ii) For this or any water control project you have studied, **describe** some of the problems caused by its development.   4

     (15)

[Turn over

Mar

Question 5: European Environmental Inequalities

Reference Map Q5A: Severe Water Pollution in Europe

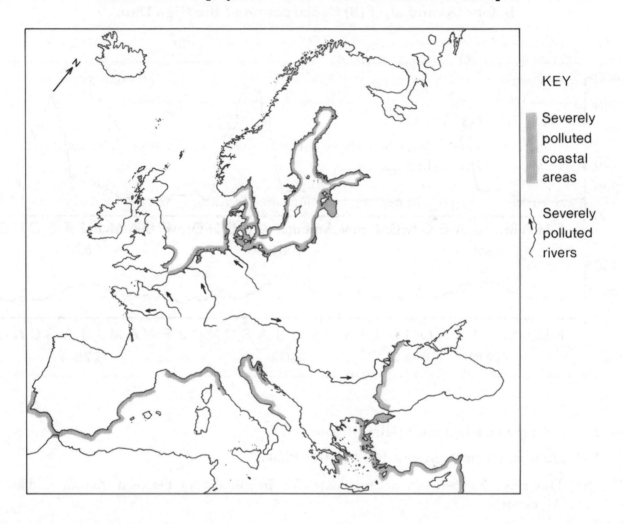

(*a*) Study Reference Map Q5A.

   (i)   Describe the distribution of severe water pollution in Europe.   **3**

   (ii) **Explain** the ways in which the development of **tourism** can pollute coastal areas.   **3**

Marks

5.   **(continued)**

Reference Diagram Q5B: Differences in Environmental Quality

> The River Rhine has often been described as "the sewer of Europe". In contrast, the River Dee in Scotland has been described as a river "with crystal clear water".

(b)   Study Reference Diagram Q5B.

Referring to the rivers described above, **or** two rivers you have studied, **explain** differences in environmental quality.   4

(c)   Choose **either** a coastal area **or** a mountainous area in Europe affected by pollution.

  (i)   **Describe** measures which governments take to improve the environmental quality of the area.

  (ii)   How successful have these measures been?   Give reasons for your answer.   5

(15)

[Turn over

Mar

Question 6: Development and Health

Reference Diagram Q6A: World GNP per Capita ($US)

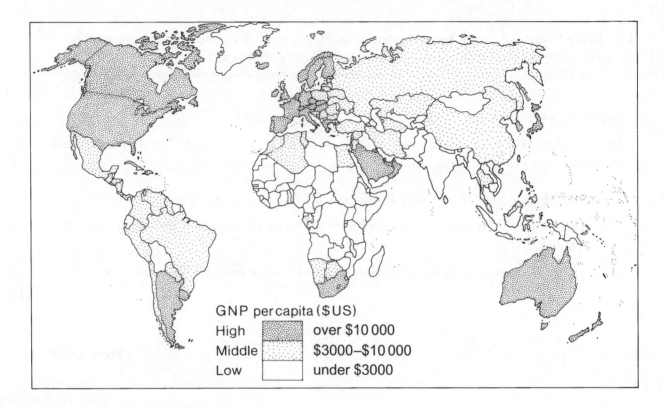

(*a*) Study Reference Diagram Q6A.

   (i) GNP per capita is **one economic** indicator of development.

   Suggest more reliable ways of comparing levels of development between different countries.   **3**

   (ii) **Explain** why some areas of the world have a higher level of development than others. You should refer to **both human and physical factors** in your answer.   **5**

(*b*) Heart disease and AIDS are two of the major health problems in Economically More Developed Countries (EMDCs).

   For **either** heart disease **or** AIDS:

   (i) **explain** the main causes of the disease;   **4**

   (ii) **describe** methods used to control or reduce the disease.   **3**

   (15)

Marks

Question 7: Environmental Hazards

Reference Diagram Q7A: Structure of a Tropical Storm

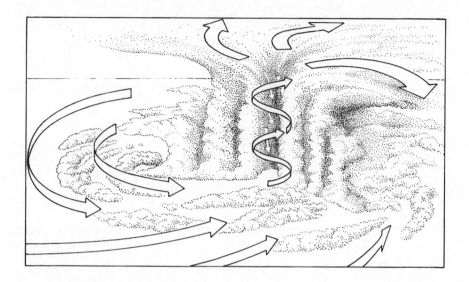

(*a*) Study Reference Diagram Q7A.

Explain in detail how tropical storms are formed.   5

Reference Diagram Q7B: World Distribution of Earthquakes and Volcanoes

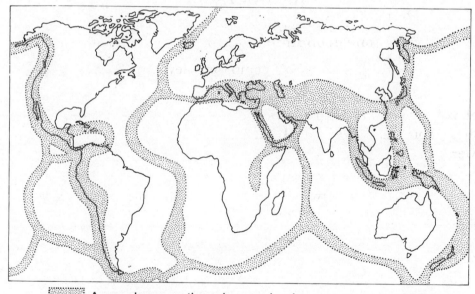

▓▓▓ Area where earthquakes and volcanoes are most likely

(*b*) Study Reference Diagram Q7B.

(i) **Explain** the world distribution of earthquakes and volcanoes.   3

(ii) **Describe** different methods of predicting tectonic activity.   4

(*c*) For any natural disaster you have studied, were methods of prediction effective?
Explain you answer.

3

(15)

[END OF QUESTION PAPER]

[BLANK PAGE]

FOR OFFICIAL USE

X208/203

NATIONAL
QUALIFICATIONS
2006

MONDAY, 29 MAY
9.00 AM – 11.00 AM

GEOGRAPHY
INTERMEDIATE 2
Worksheet Q2(b)(i)

Fill in these boxes and read what is printed below.

Full name of centre

Town

Forename(s)

Surname

Date of birth
Day Month Year

Scottish candidate number

Number of seat

To be inserted inside the front cover of the candidate's answer book
and returned with it.

WORKSHEET Q2(*b*)(i)

Pollution Levels in London and Edinburgh 1999–2003

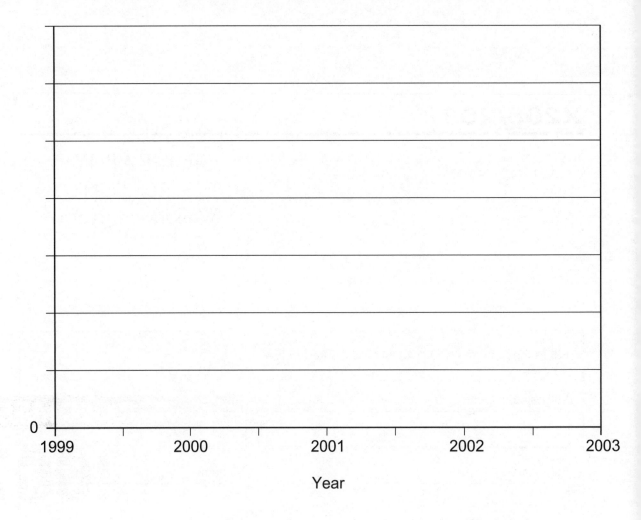

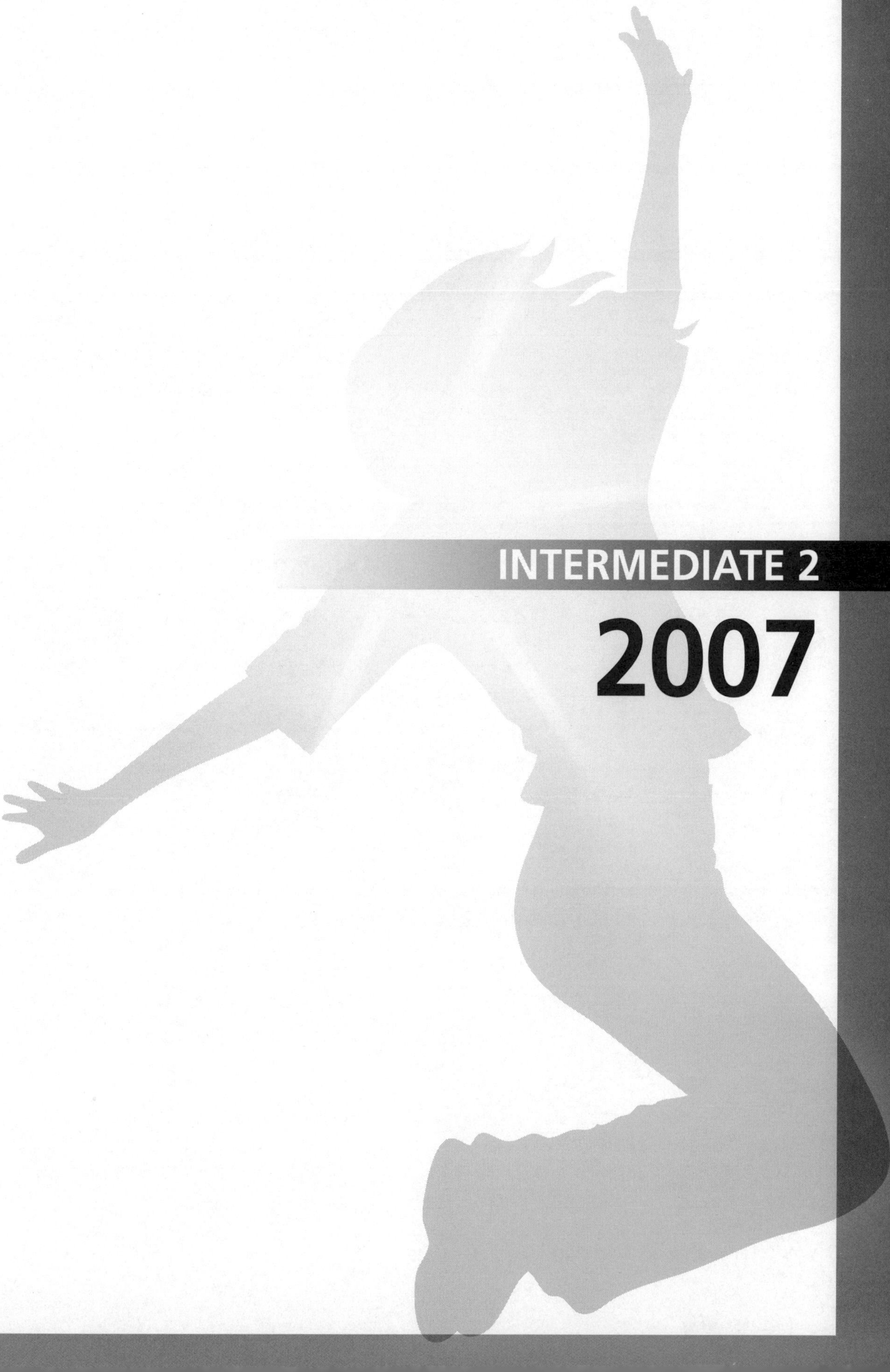

INTERMEDIATE 2

2007

[BLANK PAGE]

X208/201

NATIONAL
QUALIFICATIONS
2007

MONDAY, 28 MAY
9.00 AM – 11.00 AM

GEOGRAPHY
INTERMEDIATE 2

Candidates should answer **four** questions: Section A   Question 1
and
Question 2

AND

Section B   any **two** questions from
Questions 3 to 7

Candidates should read the questions carefully.   Answers should be clearly expressed and relevant.

Credit will always be given for appropriate sketch-maps and diagrams.

Write legibly and neatly, and leave a space of about one cm between the lines.

All maps and diagrams in this paper have been printed in black only: no other colours have been used.

SCOTTISH
QUALIFICATIONS
AUTHORITY
©

1:50 000 Scale
Landranger Series

Scale 1: 50 000
2 centimetres to 1 kilometre (one grid square)

2   1   0 Kilometres 1   2   3

1   0 Miles   1   2

1 kilometre = 0·6214 mile   1 mile = 1·6093 kilometres

Magnetic North   Grid North   True North

Diagrammatic only

Four colours should appear above; if not then please return to the invigilator.
Four colours should appear above; if not then please return to the invigilator.

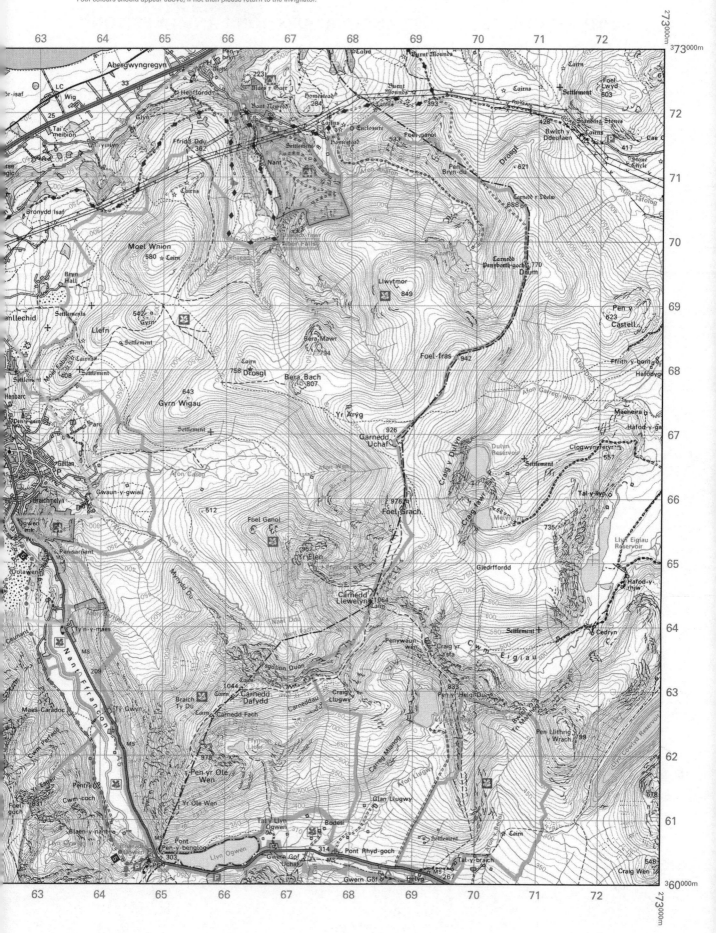

Mark

SECTION A

IN THIS SECTION YOU <u>MUST</u> ANSWER QUESTION 1 <u>AND</u> QUESTION 2.

Question 1: Physical Environments

Study the Ordnance Survey Map Extract No 1559/115.

(a) Describe the **physical** features of the river Afon Ogwen **and** its valley from grid reference 650604 to grid reference 611722.   **4**

(b) **Identify** the feature of glacial erosion found at each of the grid references below.

    662622   645610   673653   660605

Choose from:

    Corrie   Pyramidal Peak   Ribbon Lake   U-shaped Valley.   **3**

(c) **Explain** how a corrie is formed.

    You may use a diagram(s) to illustrate your answer.   **4**

Marks

1.   **(continued)**

Reference Diagram Q1A: Selected Land Uses in National Parks

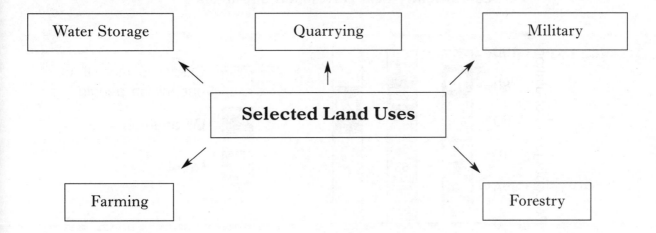

Reference Diagram Q1B: Aims of National Parks

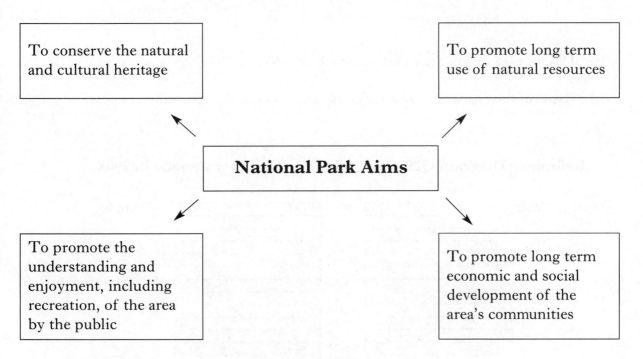

(*d*) Look at Reference Diagrams Q1A and Q1B.

Select **two** land uses from Reference Diagram Q1A.

Explain, in detail, different ways in which your chosen land uses are in conflict with the aims of the National Parks.   5

(*e*) (i) For a coastal area you have studied, **explain**, in detail, the benefits and problems which tourism has brought to the area.   5

(ii) Describe, in detail, ways in which public **and** voluntary organisations attempt to manage problems caused by tourism in such areas.   4

(25)

[END OF QUESTION 1]

NOW GO ON TO QUESTION 2

Mark

Question 2: Human Environments

Reference Diagram Q2A: Projected Changes in Urban/Rural Population for Economically Less Developed Countries

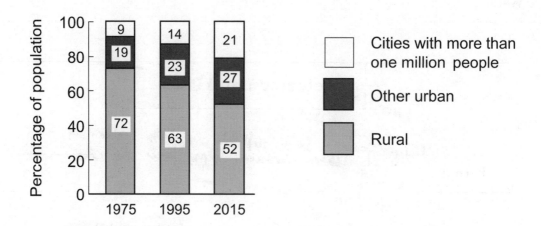

(*a*) Study Reference Diagram Q2A.

    (i)   Describe, in detail, the trends shown from 1975 to 2015.   **3**

    (ii) **Explain** the changes shown for cities with more than one million people.   **4**

Reference Diagram Q2B: Population Pyramid for Canada in 2008

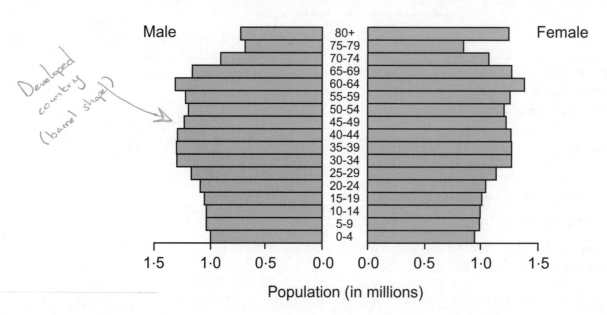

(*b*) Study Reference Diagram Q2B.

For Canada, or any other EMDC* you have studied, describe the long term problems which may be caused by its population structure.   **5**

*EMDC = *economically more developed country*

2. **(continued)**

Reference Diagram Q2C: Shopping Area, Cardiff City Centre

(*c*) Study Reference Diagram Q2C.

For a named city you have studied in an EMDC, give reasons for the main changes which have taken place in the city centre shopping area over the last thirty years.   **5**

Reference Diagram Q2D: European Agricultural Policies

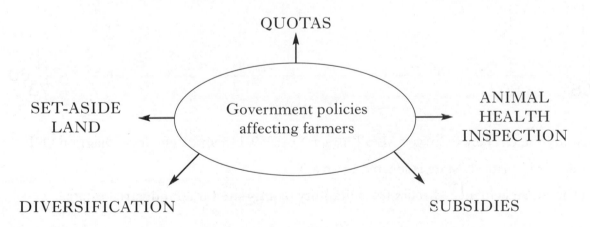

(*d*) Study Reference Diagram Q2D.

For **two** of the policies shown above, **explain** why they were necessary.   **4**

[Turn over

Mar

2.   (continued)

Reference Diagram Q2E: Bangor Industrial Estate

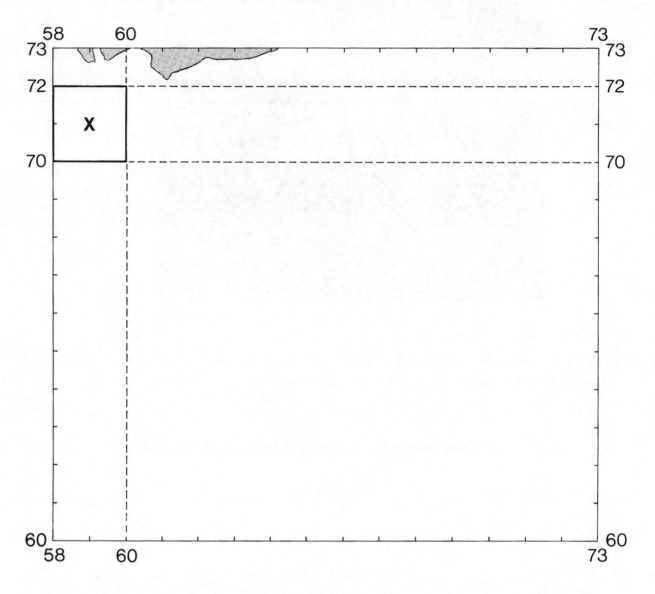

(e)   Study the Ordnance Survey Map Extract No 1559/115 and Reference Diagram Q2E.
Bangor industrial estate is located in area X.

Using map evidence, discuss the suitability of this site for an industrial estate.   **4**

(25)

[END OF SECTION A]

NOW TURN TO SECTION B AND ANSWER TWO QUESTIONS

[BLANK PAGE]

SECTION B

Environmental Interactions

Answer any two questions from this section.

Choose from

SECTION B

Marks

Question 3: Rural Land Degradation

Reference Map Q3A: Distribution of Original and Remaining Forests

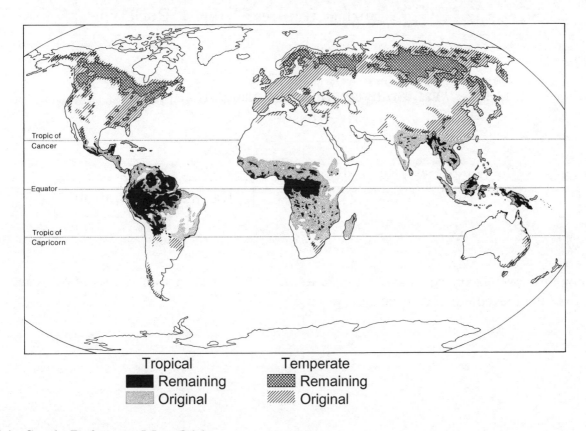

Tropical
■ Remaining
▨ Original

Temperate
▨ Remaining
▨ Original

(*a*) Study Reference Map Q3A.

For a forest area you have studied:

(i) **explain** the impact of increasing population density on the rate of deforestation;   **5**

(ii) describe ways in which the rate of deforestation can be reduced.   **4**

Reference Diagram Q3B: World Desertification

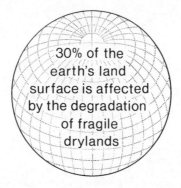

30% of the earth's land surface is affected by the degradation of fragile drylands

(*b*) Study Reference Diagram Q3B.

Describe the effects of continuing desertification on the human **and** physical environment of arid or semi-arid areas you have studied.   **6**

(15)

Mark

Question 4: River Basin Management

Reference Diagram Q4A: Factors affecting Water Movement and Storage in a River Basin

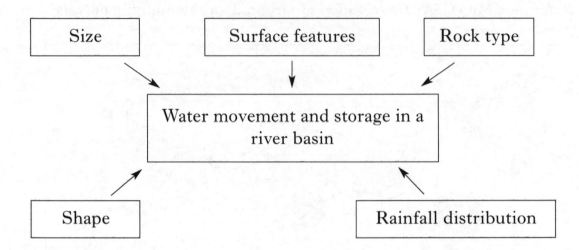

(a) For any river basin you have studied, **explain** how the factors shown above can affect the movement and storage of water.   6

Marks

4. (continued)

Reference Diagram Q4B: The Hydrological Cycle

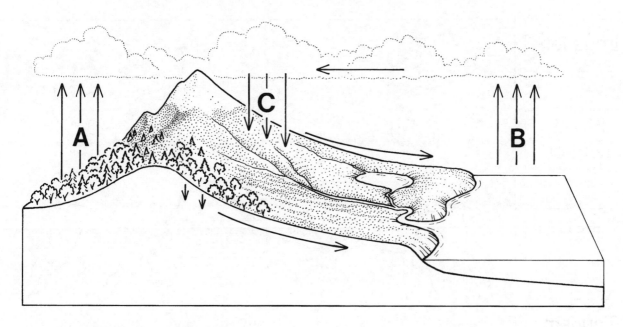

(b) Look at Reference Diagram Q4B.

Describe, in detail, the processes taking place at A, B and C. **4**

A = ?

B = Evaporation

C = Condensation

[Turn over

Mark

4. (continued)

Reference Map Q4C: Columbia River Basin Water Management

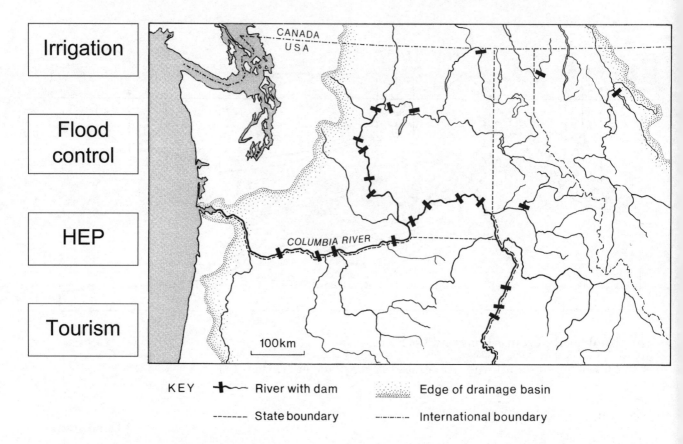

(c) Study Reference Map Q4C.

For this river basin, or any other you have studied, **explain** the benefits which a river basin management project can bring to the people and environment of the area.   **5**

(15)

Marks

Question 5: European Environmental Inequalities

Reference Map Q5A: Pattern of Acid Rain in Europe

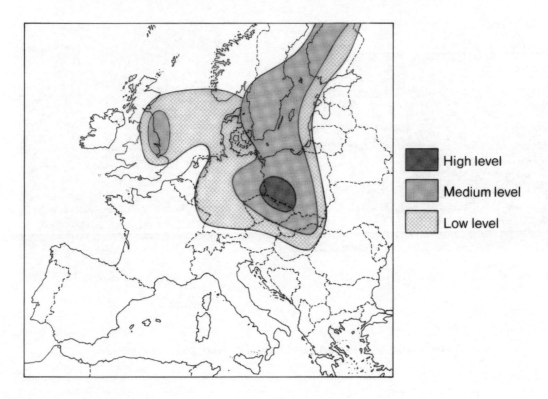

Study Reference Map Q5A.

(a) (i) Describe the variations in levels of acid rain throughout Europe. **3**

(ii) **Explain** how economic activity **and** climate affect levels of acid rain throughout Europe. **4**

[Turn over

Mar

5.   **(continued)**

Reference Diagrams Q5B(i): Coastal Areas

Magaluf

Camargue

Reference Diagrams Q5B(ii): Mountain Areas

Zermatt

North West Highlands

(*b*)   Study the photos above.

Reference Diagram Q5B(i) shows two sea/coastal areas.

Reference Diagram Q5B(ii) shows two mountain areas.

For **either** two sea/coastal areas **or** two mountain areas in Europe you have studied, **explain** the differences in their environmental quality.

You may use the examples shown if you wish.   4

(*c*)   Giving examples, describe ways in which countries and people have co-operated to improve the quality of European rivers.   4

(15)

Marks

Question 6: Development and Health

Levels of development within a country can be measured using either social or economic indicators.

(*a*) Explain why using one social **or** one economic indicator may not show a country's level of development.

5

Reference Map Q6: Worldwide Malaria Distribution in 2002

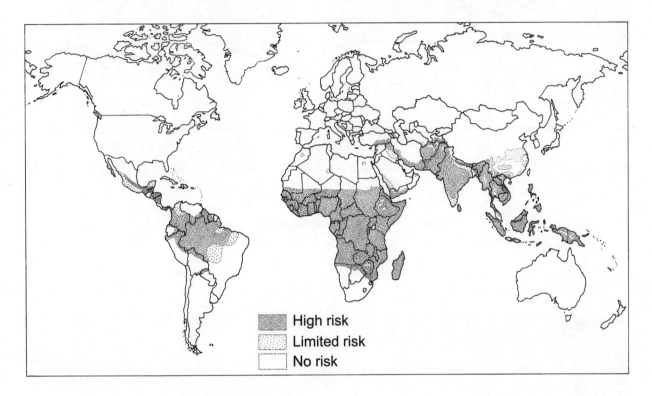

High risk
Limited risk
No risk

(*b*) Study Reference Map Q6.

Referring to the map, describe the distribution of malaria throughout the world.

3

(*c*) (i) For **either** AIDS, Malaria **or** Heart Disease, describe some of the methods used to control the disease.

4

(ii) How effective have these methods been?

3

(15)

[Turn over

Mark

Question 7: Environmental Hazards

Reference Map Q7A: Tropical Storms

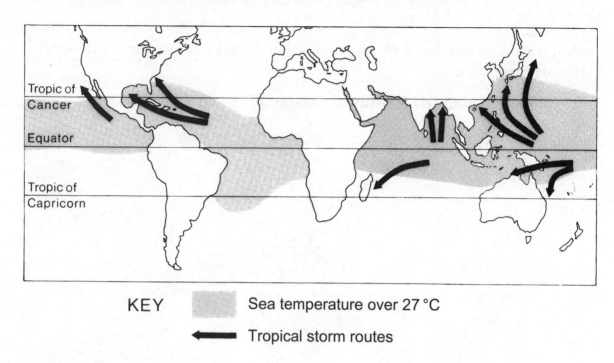

KEY   Sea temperature over 27 °C

Tropical storm routes

(*a*) Study Reference Map Q7A.

Using the information shown on the map, **explain**, in detail, the distribution of tropical storms throughout the world.   **4**

Marks

7.   (continued)

Reference Diagram Q7B: Boxing Day Tsunami 2004—Indian Ocean

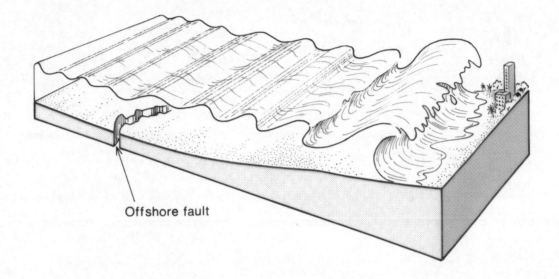

Offshore fault

(*b*) Study Reference Diagram Q7B.

> The Boxing Day tsunami was caused by a massive underwater earthquake.

(i)   Describe the effects of this, **or any other earthquake**, on the people and
surrounding areas.   **4**

(ii) For your chosen earthquake, describe the role of aid agencies involved in the
rescue operations.   **4**

(iii) How effective were their efforts?   **3**

(15)

[END OF QUESTION PAPER]

[BLANK PAGE]

2008

[BLANK PAGE]

X208/201

NATIONAL
QUALIFICATIONS
2008

THURSDAY, 22 MAY
9.00 AM – 11.00 AM

GEOGRAPHY
INTERMEDIATE 2

Candidates should answer **four** questions: Section A   Question 1
and
Question 2

AND

Section B   any **two** questions from
Questions 3 to 7

Candidates should read the questions carefully. Answers should be clearly expressed and relevant.

Credit will always be given for appropriate sketch-maps and diagrams.

Write legibly and neatly, and leave a space of about one cm between the lines.

All maps and diagrams in this paper have been printed in black only: no other colours have been used.

1:50 000 Scale
Landranger Series

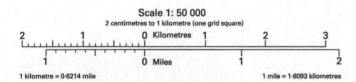

Scale 1: 50 000
2 centimetres to 1 kilometre (one grid square)

```
2          1          0  Kilometres    1          2          3
|__|__|__|__|__|__|__|__|__|__|__|__|__|__|__|__|__|__|__|__|__|
      1                0  Miles            1                2
1 kilometre = 0·6214 mile            1 mile = 1·6093 kilometres
```

Magnetic North   Grid North   True North

Diagrammatic only

Extract produced by Ordnance Survey 2007. Licence: 100035658
© Crown copyright 2004. All rights reserved.

Four colours should appear above; if not then please return to the invigilator.
Four colours should appear above; if not then please return to the invigilator.

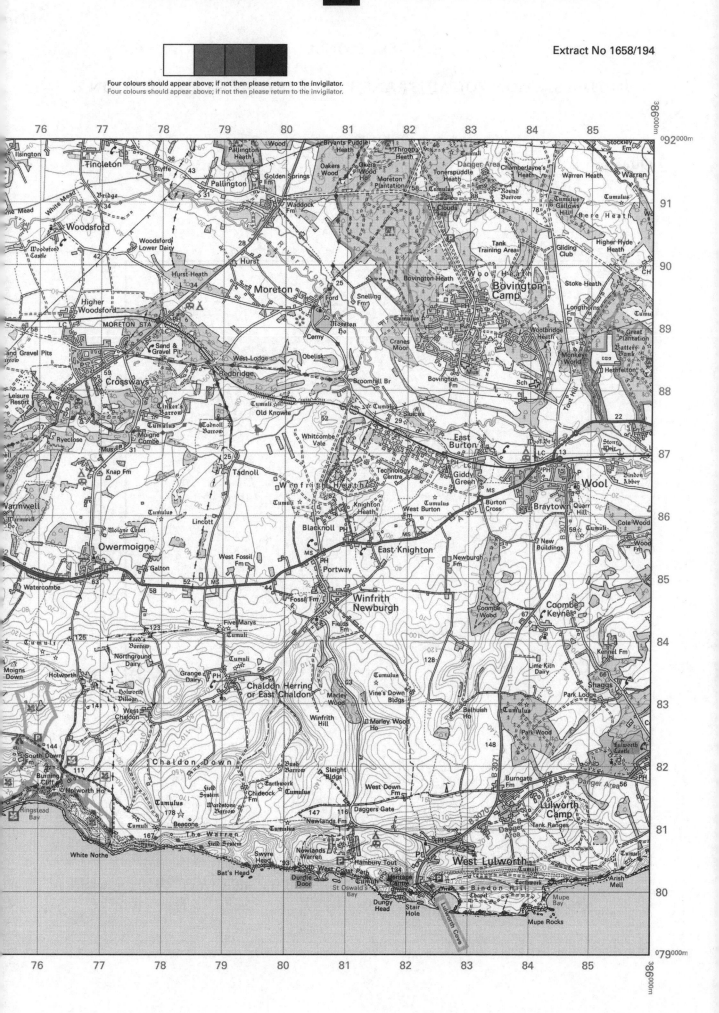

Mar

SECTION A

IN THIS SECTION YOU <u>MUST</u> ANSWER QUESTION 1 <u>AND</u> QUESTION 2.

Question 1: Physical Environments

Reference Diagram Q1A: Lulworth/Wool

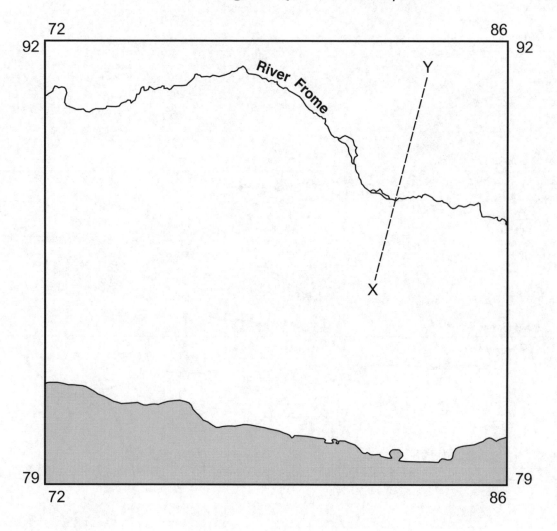

(*a*) Study the Ordnance Survey Map Extract No 1658/194 of the Lulworth/Wool area and Reference Diagram Q1A.

  (i) Choose **either** the physical coastal feature shown in 8279 **or** the physical coastal feature shown in 7780 and explain its formation in detail.

      You may wish to use diagrams in your answer.   **4**

  (ii) Describe the course of the River Frome **and** its valley from 795905 to where it leaves the map at 860867.   **4**

Marks

1. **(continued)**

Reference Diagram Q1B: Land Use Transect X–Y

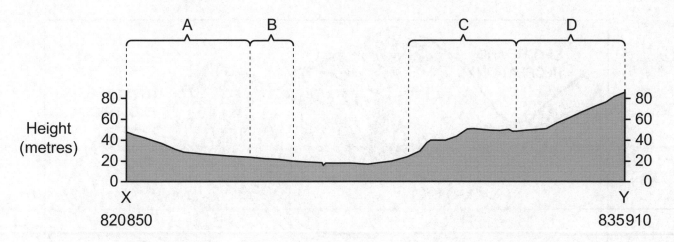

(b) Study the Ordnance Survey Map of Wool **and** Reference Diagram Q1B.

    (i) Match the letters shown on the transect X–Y above to the land uses listed below.

       Land uses: Industry;   Military Training;   Farmland;   Settlement.   **3**

    (ii) To what extent do you agree that military training activities may be in conflict with other land uses in the area of the map extract?

       Give reasons to support your answer.   **4**

[Turn over

Mar.

1.   **(continued)**

Reference Diagram Q1C: Highland Landscape

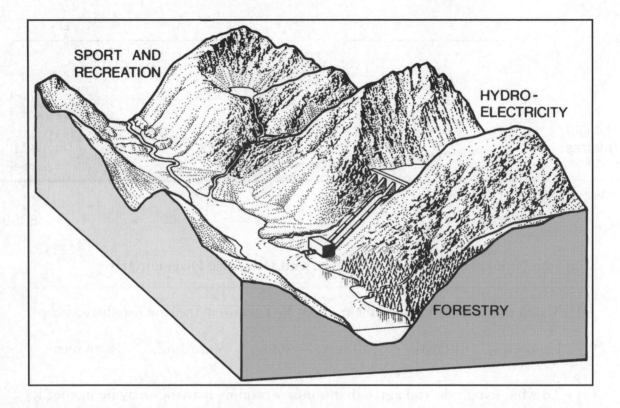

(*c*)   Study Reference Diagram Q1C.

 (i)   For **one** of the land uses shown, **explain** its economic **and** environmental impact.   6

 (ii)   Describe strategies which have been used to protect upland environments.   4

                                                                                         (25)

[END OF QUESTION 1]

NOW GO ON TO QUESTION 2

Question 2: Human Environments

Reference Diagram Q2A: World Population Density

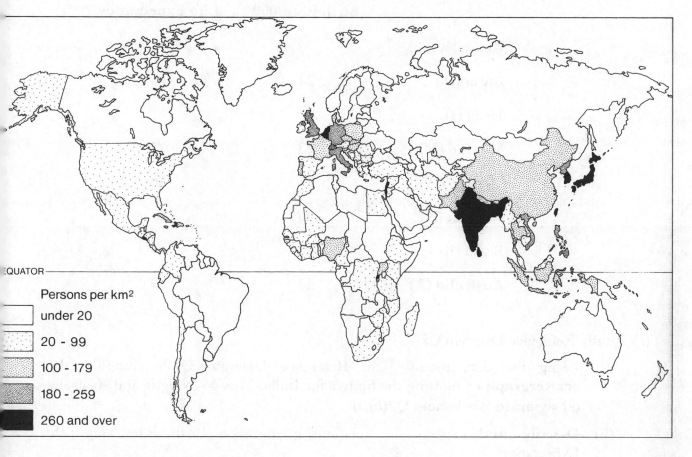

Marks

(a) Study Reference Diagram Q2A.

Referring to both physical **and** human factors, **explain** why some areas of the world have a population density of less than 20 persons per square km.

5

[Turn over

2.　(continued)

Reference Diagram Q2B:　Birth Rates and Life Expectancy

	Birth Rate/000	Life Expectancy
Kenya (K)	29	47
India (I)	**24**	**63**
Japan (J)	10	81
Mexico (M)	**23**	**72**
Canada (C)	11	80
Nigeria (N)	**40**	**51**
Brazil (B)	18	63
Australia (A)	**13**	**80**

(b)　Study Reference Diagram Q2B.

(i)　Using the data provided in Reference Diagram Q2B, complete the **scattergraph** by plotting the figures for India, Mexico, Nigeria and Australia on **separate Worksheet Q2(b)(i)**.　　2

(ii)　Describe **and** explain the relationship between Birth Rate and Life Expectancy.　　4

Reference Diagram Q2C:　Population Pyramid for Bangladesh, 2005

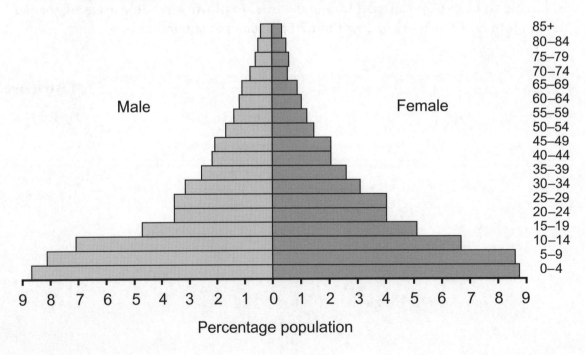

(c)　Study Reference Diagram Q2C.

What measures could countries, such as Bangladesh, take to reduce their birth rates?　　4

Marks

2. **(continued)**

Reference Diagram Q2D: A Brazilian shanty town

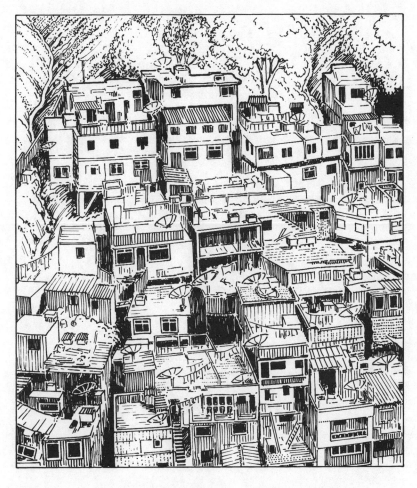

ELDC = Economically less Developed Country
EMDC = Economically More Developed Country

(*d*) For a named **ELDC** city you have studied, describe attempts made to improve living conditions in shanty towns.   **5**

(*e*) | "*During recent years the populations of many* **EMDC** *cities have decreased dramatically due to out-migration.*" |

Describe ways in which city authorities have attempted to encourage people to **move back** into their city.   **5**

    (25)

[*END OF SECTION A*]

NOW TURN TO SECTION B AND ANSWER TWO QUESTIONS

[BLANK PAGE]

SECTION B

Environmental Interactions

Answer any two questions from this section.

Choose from

Question 3	**Rural Land Degradation**	(Pages 10 to 11)
Question 4	**River Basin Management**	(Pages 12 to 13)
Question 5	**European Environmental Inequalities**	(Pages 14 to 15)
Question 6	**Development and Health**	(Page 16)
Question 7	**Environmental Hazards**	(Pages 17 to 18)

[Turn over

SECTION B

Mar

Question 3: Rural Land Degradation

Reference Diagram Q3A: Logging in Malaysia

(*a*) Study Reference Diagram Q3A.

(i) Describe the **economic** advantages of increased deforestation.   3

(ii) **Explain** ways in which deforestation affects both people **and** the environment.   4

Marks

3. **(continued)**

Reference Diagram Q3B: Desertification in Australia

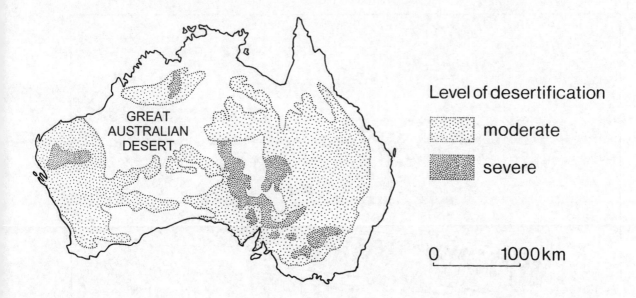

(*b*) Study Reference Diagram Q3B.

(i) **Explain** the physical **or** human causes of desertification.   **4**

(ii) For an arid or semi-arid area you have studied, describe methods used to
      reduce the desertification process.   **4**

                                                                                       (15)

[Turn over

Question 4: River Basin Management

Reference Diagram Q4A: The Mepanda Uncua Hydropower Project, Mozambique

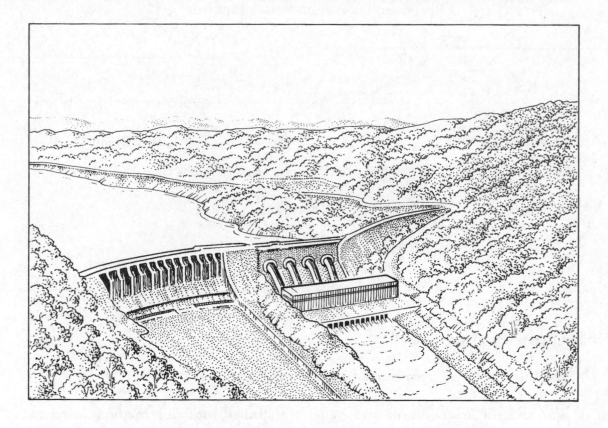

(*a*) (i) Study Reference Diagram Q4A.

For this, or any other river basin project you have studied, describe the **physical** factors which could have influenced the location of the dam.   **4**

(ii)

> ## "Local Community wants proposals for new dam stopped"

Why do some people object to the building of new dams?   **4**

4.   (continued)

Reference Diagram Q4B:
Proposed Okavango Water Pipeline

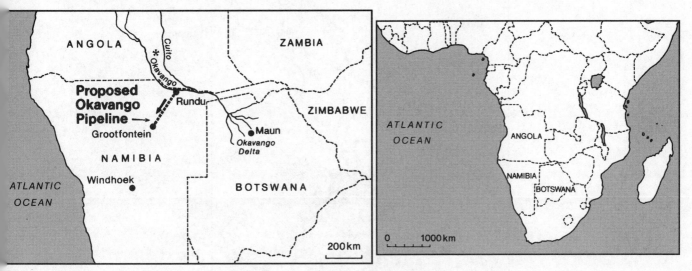

Note: * The River Okavango flows from Angola to Botswana

Reference Diagram Q4C:
Climate Graph—Grootfontein

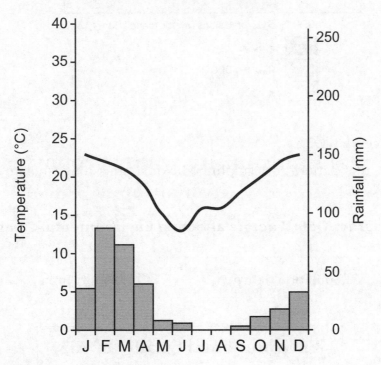

Study Reference Diagrams Q4B and Q4C.

Marks

(*b*)   (i)   What benefits could projects such as the proposed Okavango Pipeline bring to Namibia or similar areas?

4

(ii)   **Explain** why this pipeline might be a source of conflict between Namibia and Botswana.

3

(15)

Marr

Question 5: European Environmental Inequalities

Reference Map Q5A: Sulphur Dioxide (SO$_2$) Emissions in Europe

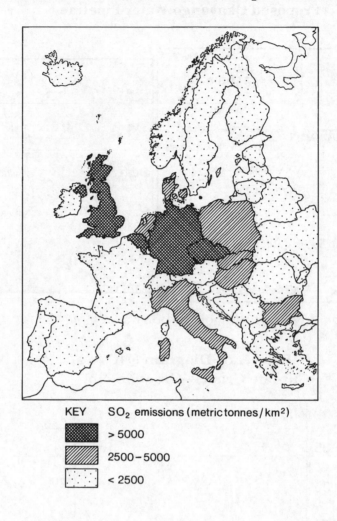

KEY   SO$_2$ emissions (metric tonnes / km^2)

> 5000

2500 – 5000

< 2500

(a) Study Reference Map Q5A.

  (i) Describe the pattern of sulphur dioxide emissions shown on Reference Map Q5A.   **4**

Reference Diagram Q5B: Factors affecting Environmental Quality of Air

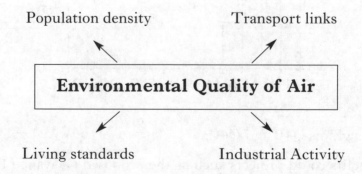

Population density   Transport links

Environmental Quality of Air

Living standards   Industrial Activity

  (ii) Give reasons for the pattern you have described in part (a)(i).

      You may refer to the factors shown in Diagram Q5B.   **4**

Marks

5. **(continued)**

Reference Diagram Q5C: European Water Supply—Key Facts

20% of all surface water is seriously threatened with pollution

Groundwater supplies 65% of all Europe's drinking water

Area of irrigated land in Southern Europe has increased by 20% since 1985

(b) Study Reference Diagram Q5C.

(i) For any river you have studied **describe** the strategies used to maintain or improve its water quality. **4**

(ii) Comment on how effective these strategies have been. **3**

(15)

[Turn over

Mark

Question 6: Development and Health

Reference Map Q6A: World Energy Consumption

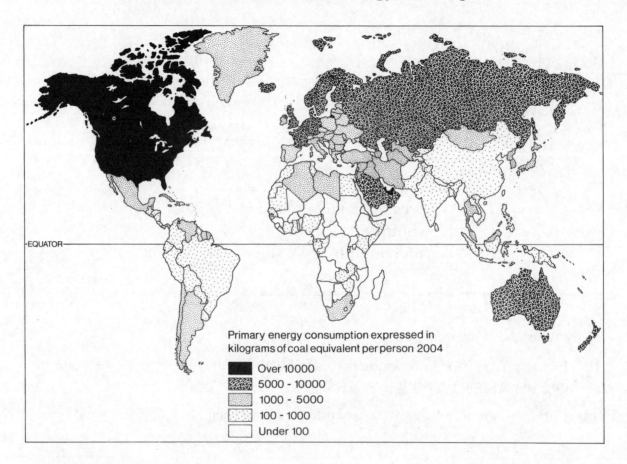

(a) Study Reference Map Q6A.

Describe the pattern of energy consumption.

4

Reference Diagram Q6B: Human Factors affecting Level of Development

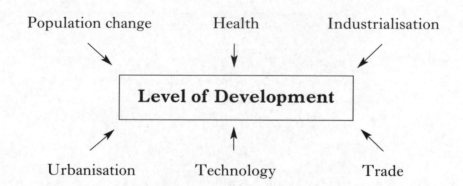

(b) Study Reference Diagram Q6B.

How do human factors such as those shown on the diagram affect the level of development of a country?

6

(c) What are the main causes of **either** malaria **or** AIDS?

5

(15)

Marks

Question 7: Environmental Hazards

Reference Map Q7A: Pakistan Earthquake, October 2005

(*a*) Study Reference Map Q7A.

For this, or any other earthquake you have studied, **explain** the main causes of the earthquake.

3

[Turn over for Questions 7(*b*) and (*c*) on *Page eighteen*

Mark

7.　**(continued)**

Reference Diagram Q7B:　Comparison of similar Richter Scale Earthquakes

Pakistan Earthquake	
October 2005	
Richter Scale	7·6
Deaths	79 000
Injured	75 038

San Francisco Earthquake	
October 1989	
Richter Scale	7·1
Deaths	63
Injured	3757

(*b*)　Study Reference Diagram Q7B.

Explain why earthquakes of similar strength have different effects on the landscape and population in the areas affected.

5

(*c*)　(i)　For a Tropical Storm you have studied, how effective were the warnings given in helping to reduce the impact of the storm?

Give reasons for your answer.

4

(ii)　What help was given to the people in the area immediately after the storm in part (*c*)(i)?

3

(15)

[END OF QUESTION PAPER]

FOR OFFICIAL USE

X208/203

NATIONAL
QUALIFICATIONS
2008

THURSDAY, 22 MAY
9.00 AM – 11.00 AM

GEOGRAPHY
INTERMEDIATE 2
Worksheet Q2(*b*)(i)

Fill in these boxes and read what is printed below.

Full name of centre

Town

Forename(s)

Surname

Date of birth
Day Month Year

Scottish candidate number

Number of seat

To be inserted inside the front cover of the candidate's answer book
and returned with it.

WORKSHEET Q2(b)(i)

SCATTERGRAPH

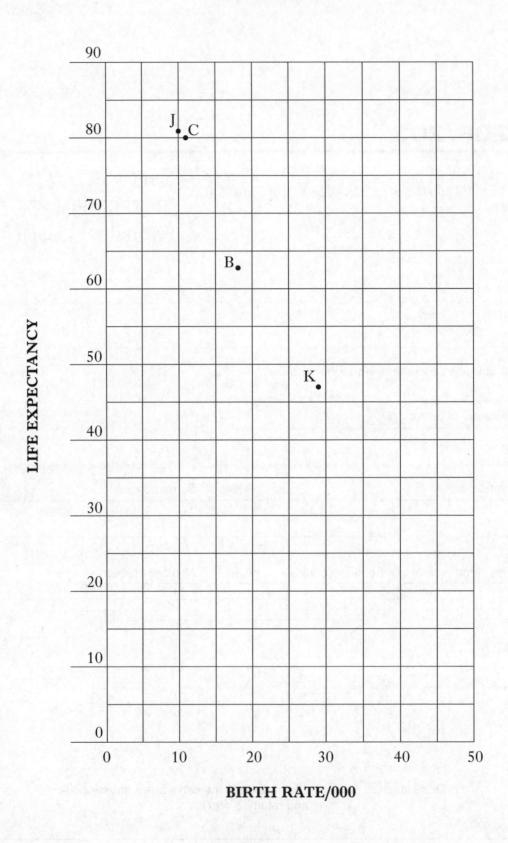

BIRTH RATE/000

[END OF WORKSHEET]

[BLANK PAGE]

X208/201

NATIONAL
QUALIFICATIONS
2009

WEDNESDAY, 27 MAY
9.00 AM – 11.00 AM

GEOGRAPHY
INTERMEDIATE 2

Candidates should answer **four** questions: Section A   Question 1
                                                                  and
                                                                  Question 2

                        AND

                        Section B   any **two** questions from
                                                                         Questions 3 to 7

Candidates should read the questions carefully. Answers should be clearly expressed and relevant.

Credit will always be given for appropriate sketch-maps and diagrams.

Write legibly and neatly, and leave a space of about one cm between the lines.

All maps and diagrams in this paper have been printed in black only: no other colours have been used.

1:25 000 Scale
Explorer Series

Four colours should appear above; if not then please return to the invigilator.

Four colours should appear above; if not then please return to the invigilator.

OL2

392⁰⁰⁰m

⁴67⁰⁰⁰m

66

65

64

63

Shake
Hole

Great
Knot

Lane

Scale 1: 25 000

4 centimetres to 1 kilometre (one grid square)

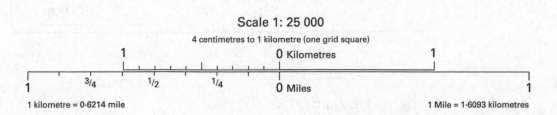

1 kilometre = 0·6214 mile   1 Mile = 1·6093 kilometres

⁴62⁰⁰⁰m

392⁰⁰⁰m

Mar

SECTION A

IN THIS SECTION YOU <u>MUST</u> ANSWER QUESTION 1 <u>AND</u> QUESTION 2.

Question 1: Physical Environments

Reference Diagram Q1A

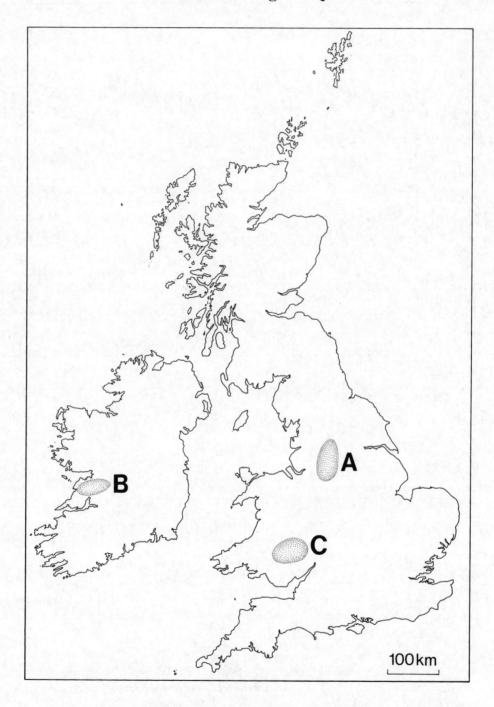

100 km

(*a*) Look at Reference Diagram Q1A.

Name the **three** areas of upland limestone shown on the map.

3

Marks

1. **(continued)**

(*b*) Study the Ordnance Survey Map Extract (No 1744/OL2).

    (i) Match each of the following landscape features found on the map with the correct grid reference.

      Limestone pavement   **Gorge**   **Shake Hole**   **Pot Holes**

      Choose from:

      Grid References   872662   914638   903647   873647   906654.   **4**

    (ii) For **one** of the features mentioned above, **explain** how it was formed.

      You may wish to use a diagram(s) in your answer.   **4**

Reference Diagram Q1B

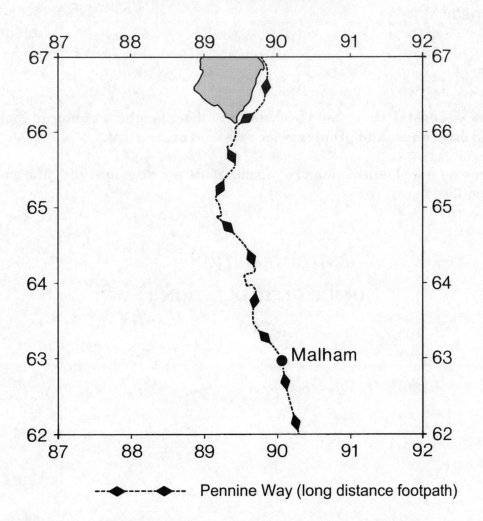

- - -◆- - - - -◆- - - Pennine Way (long distance footpath)

    (iii) Study the Ordnance Survey Map Extract (No 1744/OL2) and Reference Diagram Q1B.

      Explain why this is a suitable route for the Pennine Way.   **4**

Mark

1. **(continued)**

Reference Diagram Q1C

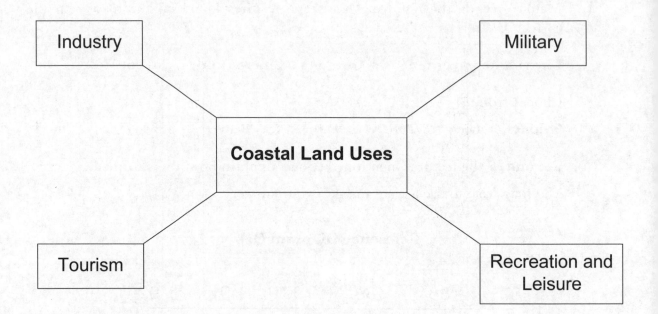

(c) (i) Select any **two** of the above land uses.

For a **coastal** area you have studied, describe the **economic benefits** and **environmental problems** for each land use selected.   **6**

(ii) How do public **and** voluntary organisations try to reduce the problems you identified in part (i)?   **4**

(25)

[END OF QUESTION 1]

NOW GO ON TO QUESTION 2

Marks

Question 2: Human Environments

Reference Diagram Q2A: Population Pyramids for an Economically Less Developed Country (ELDC)

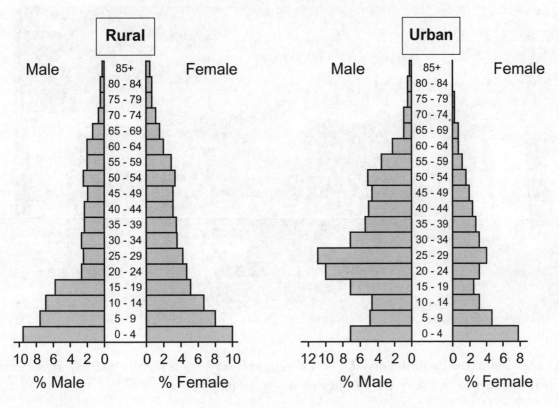

(a) Look at Reference Diagram Q2A.

   (i)   Describe the main **differences** in the population structures between the **rural** and **urban** areas, shown in Reference Diagram Q2A, in an ELDC. **3**

   (ii) Suggest reasons for the differences you described in (a)(i). **4**

Reference Diagram Q2B: Infant Mortality Statistics

Country	Infant Mortality per 1000 live Births
USA	6
UK	5
India	54
Bangladesh	60

(b) **Explain** why Economically More Developed Countries (EMDCs) have a low infant mortality rate. **3**

[Turn over

Mark

2. **(continued)**

Reference Diagram Q2C

(c) For any named Economically Less Developed city you have studied, describe measures taken to improve the quality of life in shanty towns.   **5**

Reference Diagram Q2D: Recent Changes in Agriculture in Economically Less Developed Countries (ELDCs)

Increased use of Chemical fertilisers	Increased Mechanisation

(d) What benefits **and** problems have changes such as those shown in the diagram brought to ELDCs?   **5**

Marks

2. **(continued)**

Reference Diagram Q2E: Nueva Condomina—Murcia in Spain

The shopping centre includes a 15 screen multiplex and a $13\,700\,m^2$ Hypermarket. There is parking for 6500 cars.

(*e*) What are the advantages **and** disadvantages of this or any other Edge of Town shopping development you have studied?

5

(25)

[END OF SECTION A]

NOW TURN TO SECTION B AND ANSWER TWO QUESTIONS

[BLANK PAGE]

SECTION B

Environmental Interactions

Answer any two questions from this section.

Choose from

[Turn over

SECTION B

Mar

Question 3: Rural Land Degradation

Reference Diagram Q3A: Sokoto, Nigeria Location

Reference Diagram Q3B: Sokoto, Niger Climate

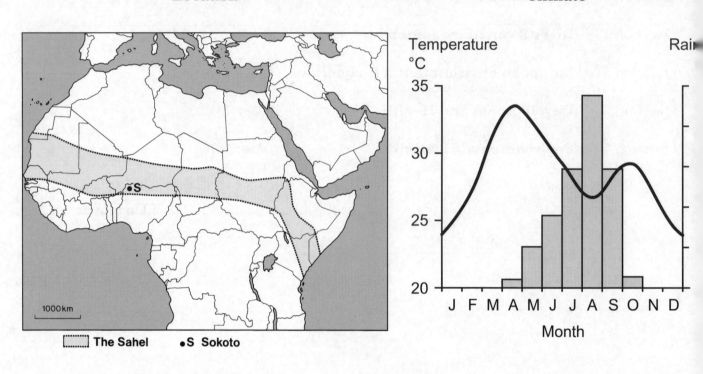

The Sahel   ●S Sokoto

(a) (i) Study Reference Diagrams Q3A and Q3B above.

Explain why the climate of Sokoto might cause desertification in the surrounding area.

3

Marks

3. **(a) (continued)**

Reference Diagram Q3C: Desertification

(ii) Study Reference Diagram Q3C.

Some countries are trying to reduce desertification.

(a) Describe the methods used.

(b) Do you think these methods are successful?

Explain your answer.   4

(b) (i) For a forested area you have studied, describe how farming can lead to land
degradation.   4

(ii) Describe what can be done to prevent deforestation.   4

(15)

[Turn over

Question 4: River Basin Management

Reference Diagram Q4A: Physical Characteristics of a River Basin

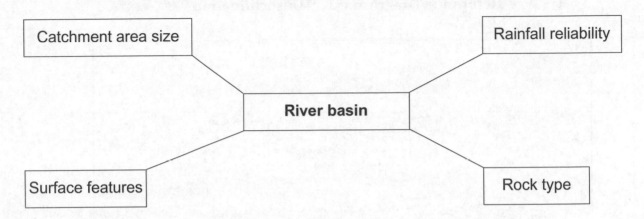

(a) Study Reference Diagram Q4A.

Why are some river basins better suited to water management projects than others?

Reference Diagram Q4B: Nile River Basin

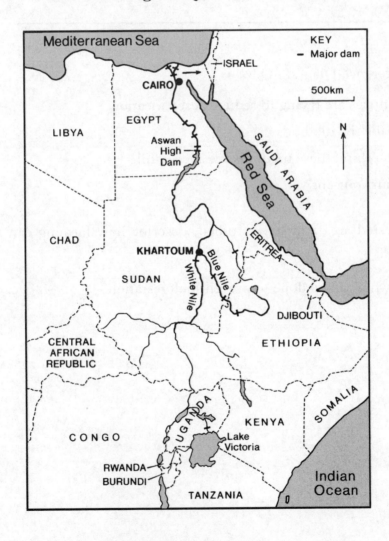

(b) Study Reference Diagram Q4B.

For the Nile River basin, or any other river you have studied, what are the benefits of managing the river?

Marks

4.   (continued)

Reference Diagram Q4C: Murray–Darling River Basin

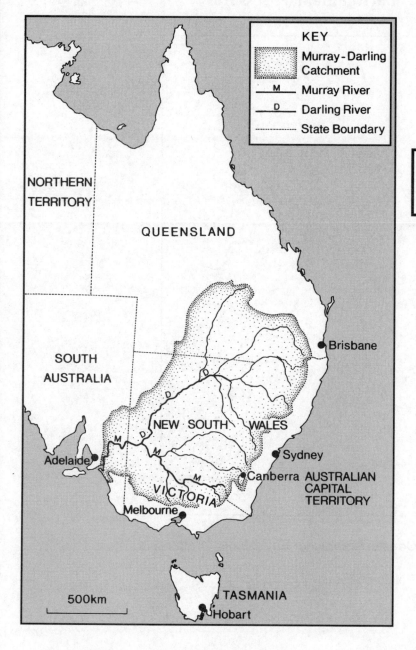

KEY

Murray – Darling Catchment

M Murray River

D Darling River

State Boundary

NORTHERN TERRITORY

QUEENSLAND

SOUTH AUSTRALIA

NEW SOUTH WALES

Brisbane

Adelaide

Sydney

Canberra AUSTRALIAN CAPITAL TERRITORY

VICTORIA

Melbourne

500km

TASMANIA

Hobart

2,000,000 householders live in the Murray–Darling river basin area.

(c) Study Reference Diagram Q4C.

   (i) What factors, other than household use, can increase the demand for water? Give reasons for your answer.   **4**

   (ii) Water control projects can cause political problems. Describe some of these problems.   **3**

(15)

[Turn over

Mar

Question 5: European Environmental Inequalities

Reference Map Q5A: Selected European Coastal Areas and Rivers under Environmental Pressure

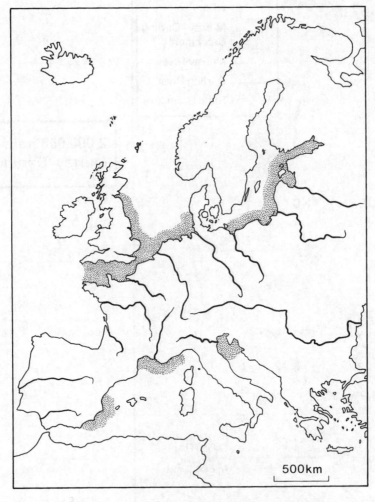

Key　　Coastal Area under Environmental Pressure

　Polluted Rivers

(*a*)　Study Reference Map Q5A.

Coastal areas are under increasing environmental pressure.

Referring to economic **and** social factors, **explain** why such areas are under threat.　5

(*b*)　For any **two** rivers you have studied, **explain** differences in their environmental quality.　3

(*c*)　(i)　What methods have been used to improve environmental quality in either a coastal or mountain area you have studied?　4

　　(ii)　Have these methods been successful?

　　　Give reasons for your answer.　3

(15

Marks

Question 6: Development and Health

Reference Diagram Q6A: Levels of Wealth and Life Expectancy

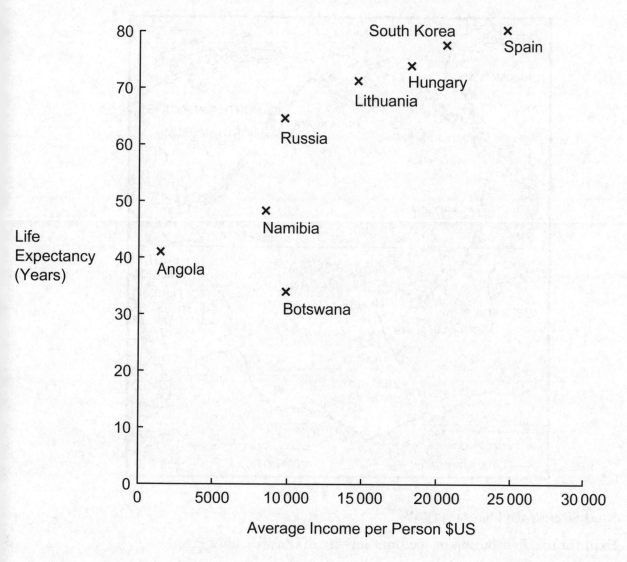

(a) Study Reference Diagram Q6A.

(i) Describe **in detail** the relationship between average income and life expectancy.   **3**

(ii) Why are combined indicators such as the Human Development Index (HDI) more reliable methods of measuring a country's overall level of development?   **4**

(b) (i) For heart disease **or** malaria, what are the consequences of the disease for the population in an affected area?   **4**

(ii) For the disease chosen in (b)(i), how successful are the methods used to control it?

Explain your answer.   **4**

(15)

[Turn over

Mar.

Question 7: Environmental Hazards

Reference Diagram Q7A: Pacific Ring of Fire

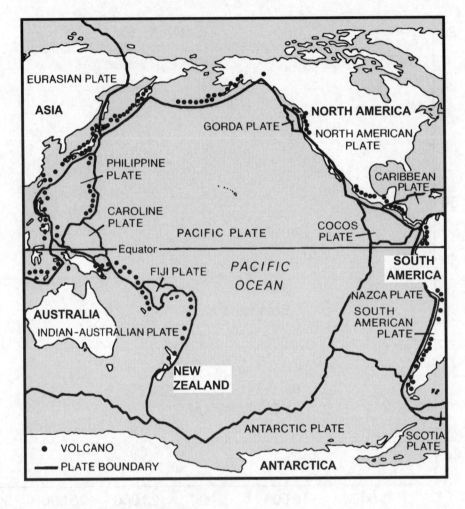

(a) Study Reference Diagram Q7A.

Explain the distribution of tectonic activity in the area shown.   3

(b) Referring to an earthquake **or** volcanic eruption you have studied:

   (i)   describe methods of predicting the hazard;   3

   (ii) **explain** the importance of both short term **and** long term aid in reducing the effects of the hazard.   4

(c) For a named tropical storm you have studied, describe **in detail** its impact on the landscape **and** population.   5

(15

[END OF QUESTION PAPER]

[BLANK PAGE]

Acknowledgements

Permission has been sought from all relevant copyright holders and Bright Red Publishing is grateful for the use of the following:

A map and population pyramid for Bangladesh taken from 'The New Wider World' by David Waugh. Reproduced with permission (2008 pages 5 & 6);

A drawing of a Brazilian Shanty Town from 'Geography Matters (Scotland) 1' by John Hopkin. Published by Heinemann Educational Publishers 2002 (2008 page 7);

Ordnance Survey © Crown Copyright. All rights reserved. Licence number 100049324.